Hands-On Science Fun

How to Make

SLIME

Revised Edition

by Lori Shores

Consultant: Ronald Browne, PhD
Department of Elementary & Early Childhood Education
Minnesota State University, Mankato

CAPSTONE PRESS
a capstone imprint

Download the
Capstone 4D app
for additional content.

 See page 2
for directions.

Download the Capstone 4D app!

- Ask an adult to search in the Apple App Store or Google Play for "Capstone 4D".
- Click Install (Android) or Get, then Install (Apple).
- Open the app.
- Scan any of the following spreads with this icon:

When you scan a spread, you'll find fun extra stuff to go with this book!
You can also find these things on the web at www.capstone4D.com
using the password: **slime.09427**

Pebble Plus is published by Capstone Press,
1710 Roe Crest Drive, North Mankato, Minnesota 56003
www.mycapstone.com

Library of Congress Cataloging-in-Publication Data
is available on the Library of Congress website.

ISBN 978-1-5435-0942-7 (library binding)
ISBN 978-1-5435-0948-9 (paperback)
ISBN 978-1-5435-0954-0 (ebook pdf)

Editorial Credits
Marissa Kirkman, editor; Sarah Bennett, designer;
Tracy Cummins, media researcher; Tori Abraham,
production specialist

Photo Credits
Capstone Studio/Karon Dubke: Cover, 1, 3, 4, 5, 7, 9, 11, 13, 15,
17, 19, 21

Note to Parents and Teachers

The Hands-On Science Fun set supports national science
standards related to physical science. This book describes and
illustrates making slime. The images support early readers
in understanding the text. The repetition of words and
phrases helps early readers learn new words. This book also
introduces early readers to subject-specific vocabulary words,
which are defined in the Glossary section. Early readers may
need assistance to read some words and to use the Table of
Contents, Glossary, Read More, Internet Sites, Critical Thinking
Questions, and Index sections of the book.

Printed and bound in the United States of America.
010772S18

Table of Contents

Safety Note:
Please ask an adult for help when making slime.

Getting Started

What's runny like glue,

but also hard like rubber?

Slime! It feels like a solid

and a liquid at the same time.

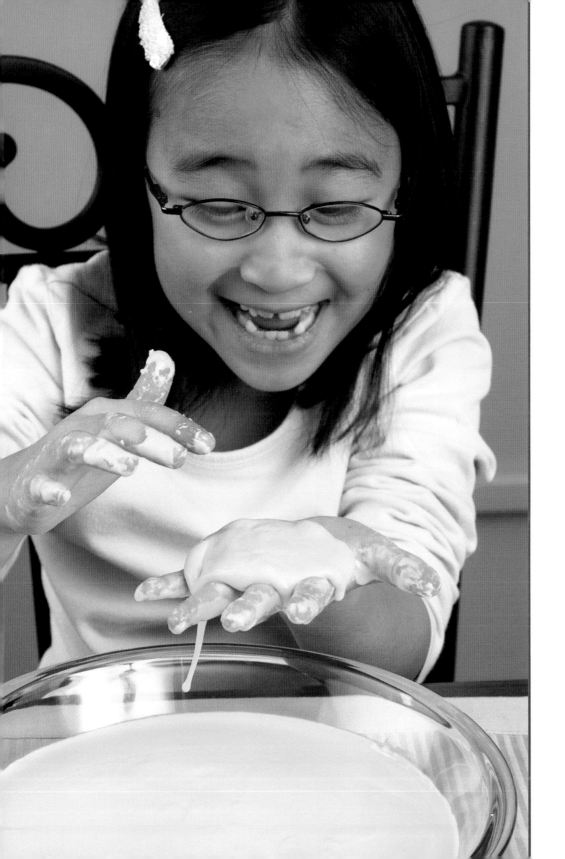

Here's what you need:

dish

food coloring

1 cup (240 mL)
cornstarch

spoon

½ cup (120 mL) water

5

Making Slime

Put ½ cup water
in a large dish.

Add a few drops
of green food coloring.

Add 1 cup of cornstarch
a little at a time.

Stir the mixture well
with a spoon.

The slime should tear
when stirred quickly.

If it doesn't tear, add
a little more cornstarch
one spoonful at a time.

Gently rest your hand
on top of the slime.

Then quickly slap
the surface of the slime.

What happens?

Try making a slime ball.

Push on it as you roll it
in your hands.

What happens when
you let go?

How Does It Work?

Water and cornstarch don't mix completely. The slime is mostly tightly packed bits of cornstarch. The water flows around those bits.

When your hand moves

slowly through the slime,

the cornstarch moves around.

The water flows and the slime

seems like a liquid.

When you slap the slime,
the cornstarch doesn't have time
to move. The water can't flow,
and the slime feels solid.

Glossary

cornstarch—a flour-like ingredient made from corn

liquid—a wet substance that can be poured

mixture—something made up of different things mixed together

rubber—a strong, elastic substance used to make items such as tires, balls, and boots

solid—a substance that holds its shape

surface—the top part of something

Read More

Heinecke, Liz Lee. *Kitchen Science Lab for Kids: 52 Family-Friendly Experiments From Around the House.* Beverly, Mass.: Quarry Books, 2014.

Huffman, Julie. *101 Ways to Gross Out Your Friends.* Lake Forest, Calif.: Quarto Publishing Group, 2016.

Miller, Rachel, Holly Homer, and Jamie Harrington. *The 101 Coolest Simple Science Experiments.* Salem, Mass.: Page Street Publishing Co., 2016.

Internet Sites

Use FactHound to find Internet sites related to this book.

Visit *www.facthound.com*

Just type **9781543509427** and go.

Super-cool stuff!

Check out projects, games and lots more at
www.capstonekids.com

Critical Thinking Questions

1. Why does the water flow around the tightly packed bits of cornstarch?

2. What happens to the cornstarch and the water when your hand moves slowly through the slime?

3. Why does the slime feel solid when you quickly slap your hand on the surface of the slime?

Index